WHAT
GOD
SEES

LOOKING AT LIFE FROM A
HEAVENLY PERSPECTIVE

BRENDA G. RIDING

HigherLife Publishing
Oviedo, FL

HigherLife Development Services, Inc.,
PO Box 623307, Oviedo, FL 32762
(407) 563–4806, higherlifepublishing.com

Published 2025
Printed in the United States of America

ISBN: 978-1-964081-62-5 (paperback)
ISBN: 978-1-964081-63-2 (ebook)
Copyright Case Number: 1–14943285061

Dedication

To my husband, Paul, the greatest man I've ever met.
And, of course, to Him who is all—my Lord and Savior, Jesus.

In Memory of

My precious, three-legged friend, Peg.
She will be missed.

Contents

Introduction

The world is a scary and stressful place. Every day seems to present something new to fear or worry about. But when the world hits hard—when the news overwhelms or sadness creeps in—I've found it helps to step back and remember what's still good.

How often do you stop to ask, "What am I thankful for?" It's a powerful question. We take so much for granted—our homes, our health, our families, and our daily comforts. Many of these blessings come through people—parents, friends, co-workers, even strangers—but, ultimately, they come from God Himself.

Matthew 5:45 says, *"He causes His sun to rise on the evil and the good, and sends rain on the righteous and the unrighteous"* (NASB). What separates the righteous from the unrighteous is not what *we* do—but the forgiveness of God. That verse reminds me that God is generous to all of us, not because we deserve it but because He is good.

One morning during my Bible study, I felt the weight of the world's chaos—wars, disasters, hate, division. I decided to push back, to give thanks, to look for good, to notice the blessings I'd overlooked. And I committed to posting something every day on social media to remind myself—and anyone who'd read it—that God is still here, still good, still faithful.

That's how this book was born. It's a collection of things I've chosen to be thankful for. A few, I hope, will surprise you—or cause you to see them from a different angle. Some are serious, some simple, some just plain silly. But each one is true. When we decide—every day—to be thankful for *something*, life's just better.

So come sit with me for a bit. Let's remember what we've been given. Let's laugh a little. Let's take one more look at the world—not as it seems—but as *God sees it.*

Rainbows

THANK GOD FOR RAIN. WE need water from the sky, even if it spoils our picnic. Rainbows—so amazing to see—only come with water. Let me tell you my story.

When my husband and I lived in Germany, we had a small apartment in the middle of farmland. At the time, I had no car, no phone, no television, no friends, and no one to talk to. Not even a pet.

I started feeling sorry for myself.

One cloudy, rainy, miserable day, I was all alone feeling depressed, abandoned, lost, and confused. I prayed, complaining to God about all my woes. Almost as soon as I said, "Amen," the rain stopped, the clouds broke, and an absolutely gorgeous rainbow appeared with its bow ending in my own backyard!

I heard God's voice inside saying that He was with me, would always be with me, and to start counting the ways I was blessed. I soared from deep depression to the highest of joys—and that rainbow? It stayed in the sky and in my backyard for quite a few minutes.

He never leaves, never forsakes, never forgets.

The rainbow is a reminder of His mercy. Look up Hosea 6:3. Now, whenever I see a rainbow, I remember God's promise to always be with us—no matter what we're going through.

Soap

THERE'S NOTHING I ENJOY MORE than a hot bath—to just sit and soak and read a book or magazine. Sadly, the older I get, the harder it becomes to get in and out of the tub. I worry about falling. At my age any fall can be dangerous, so, now my pleasure comes from just standing in a hot shower.

But what's a shower without soap?
Just water.

I love those extra-luxurious kinds of soap that turn a "get-it-done-quick" shower into a moment of pause, of quiet, of thankfulness—even luxury.

Clean water—hot or cold—is a miracle in itself. But scented soap? Lavender, citrus, rose, lemon, mint. So many choices, scents, and colors! When I have those, I don't only feel clean but pampered. Blessed.

And shampooing my hair, massaging the soap into a lather, feeling the hot water run all the suds out—is bliss. It just feels good.

Sadly, many people in the world today don't even have clean, safe water to bathe in or drink. We are blessed in this country with hot water and lovely scented soap. Give thanks to God above that you can enjoy being clean and fresh—and maybe even pampered—every day.

Scary Place

THE WORLD IS A SCARY and stressful place. Every day seems to present something new to be scared or worried about. But when the world hits you hard and things go wrong, when the news terrifies and saddens you, step back and focus on all the good things. Instead of only seeing what's wrong and scary, be thankful for what's right and good.

We take so much for granted. Yet so much of what we have is given to us by our parents, family, friends, employers, government, but most of all, by God Himself. As Matthew 5:45 says, *"He causes His sun to rise on the evil and the good, and sends rain on the righteous and the unrighteous"* (NASB). And what separates the righteous from the unrighteous? God's forgiveness.

Jesus lived as a normal, poor human in a conquered country for thirty-three years. He was born into this world as helpless as any of us. He grew up like us. Experienced life like us. He died a death so horrible most of us can't even imagine it. And why? So that we can't say, "He doesn't understand." He does, both the best and the worst things in life.

Thank You, Holy Spirit, for guiding, forgiving, and for helping me and all who trust in You to survive the day, no matter what.

Have a blessed day. And if it's not? Well, tomorrow's another day.

A New Day

I'T'S A NEW DAY. HAVE you given God thanks for that? Even if the day is not perfect, or it took a bit of effort to get out of bed, still, I'm thankful. The sun rose and I hope to see the stars tonight. God is good even when people aren't. I have another day to spend with my husband, family, and friends, to let others know how good God is. I'm thankful for today, whatever it brings.

Sometimes I think we go through life with a dark cloud raining on our heads. But they say (and I think "they're" right) that laughter is the best medicine. When things go wrong, decide to laugh instead of fussing. Unless it's life threatening, it really doesn't matter.

Once, I was in a church group and shared that I liked to dance with my husband. There was a strange silence until one friend asked, "Did you just say you like to pole dance?"

My face burned hot. "No, no!" I quickly exclaimed. "I like *Paul*. Dancing with Paul." Everybody laughed.

Truth is, when you don't feel like laughing is usually when you need it most. Determine today to look for the funny in all that happens. Tell a joke. Watch your pets. Laugh. No matter what.

Ice

WHERE I LIVE IN VIRGINIA, we enjoy four distinct seasons. I remember as a child spring bursting out with life as plants bloomed, animals appeared, and birds set up a concert. In summer, school was out—but it got *hot* and always came with a sunburn. My favorite was autumn. The heat of summer was done, and you wore layers to keep the frosty out. But after that was winter with its ice and snow.

I am thankful for ice and snow.

Okay, calm down, I can hear you yelling. You're thinking: *Yes, snow is beautiful to watch as it falls and makes the world silent—until you have to go out in it!*

Slip, slide, whether on foot or in a vehicle, ice shows up uninvited. The snow slows everything down and causes accidents.

But many people love snow and ice. Skiers, ice skaters, sled riders, people who take frosty-air walks in the woods—all children when school is cancelled.

Ice and cold also protect and preserve. Without the cold, food spoils quickly. And if you pull a muscle, our bodies need the cold of ice to numb the pain, ease the swelling, and pull inflammation out like a thief in reverse.

Snow and ice make us slow down, and sometimes, we really need to.

So, I am thankful that we have a time of rest, of quiet, of ice and snow, to slow us down.

Clouds and Wind

I'VE ALWAYS LOVED THE WIND and clouds. As a child, I would lie in the grass, stare up at the sky, and peek through the leaves of the big oak tree. I adored the wind and would "race" it, convinced I could leap high enough for it to catch me and let me fly!

Everyone remembers pointing out shapes in clouds.

"Look, it's a dog!" or, "That's a ship."

Even storm clouds have a certain beauty, as long as they're far away. The painter J. M. W. Turner shared my passion for clouds—his paintings often feature big, fluffy formations.

Of course, clouds can bring thunderstorms, which provide necessary rain but also lightning and damage. Wind, too, can be destructive. Hurricanes and tornadoes can wipe out entire towns.

Still, I cherish the gentle breeze that kisses my cheek, the soft winds carrying the scent of flowers, and the stronger gusts that blow away my troubles. I love the ever-changing clouds that provide shade from the sun and bring much-needed rain.

Clouds and wind remind me of God the Holy Spirit, who is unseen yet guides us. Like the wind and clouds, He is always present, and when we seek Him, we find Him.

That's another reason I love clouds and wind—they symbolize God's constant presence.

Another New Day

EVERY DAY I FALL OUT of bed and—glad I haven't hurt myself—I thank God that I am able to do so. Then, I check in with a few questions:

Who am I?
Where am I?
And what do I have to do today?

If I remember all of that, I know it will be a good day.

When I was younger, I never gave a thought to thanking God for being able to jump out of bed and get on with my life. Instead, I usually groaned about having to get up to go to school, and later, work. The older we grow and the more we experience all that life gives us, the good and the bad, the more we appreciate simple things and realize how valuable time and people are.

But it's so *easy* to complain, I know. That's one reason I started posting encouraging comments on Facebook—to remind us of all the good we have instead of just grumbling.

Be grateful. It's healthy. Look around, maybe before you fall out of bed. Thank God for all that you do have, and all you can do. Remember that old saying, "Accentuate the positive." Give thanks in all things. That's my motto. Hope it's yours too, at least for today.

Bugs

I THANK GOD FOR BUGS. I am so thankful—

Okay, not really. Some bugs I like—ladybugs, praying mantis, honeybees—but most I tolerate. And a few I really, really hate—mosquitoes, fleas, ticks, cockroaches—*ugh*. But they were created and serve a purpose (food for birds?). Even spiders have a purpose (to eat other bugs).

We live in a fallen world, which includes many nasty things, like the billion insects. But if all the bugs in the world suddenly disappeared, so would many good things, like birds and flowers and honey and . . . probably more than I can imagine.

I've even heard that bugs help keep the earth in balance—pollinating, cleaning, feeding other creatures. That doesn't mean I want them crawling on my ceiling at night. Nope. But it does remind me that God can and does use even the worst parts of life to do something good.

Bugs remind me that not everything I don't like is useless. Even cow poop turns into fertilizer that makes the plants and fruit trees grow better. Some things we want gone might actually be holding it all together—even putting food on your table.

So, if and when you see an insect, thank God for it. And if it's in your house, **SQUASH IT!!!**

Red Light

WHEN THE LIGHT SWITCHED FASTER than I expected from yellow to red, I slammed on the brakes. I'm so glad I had working brakes and that nobody was too close behind me, speeding to get through the yellow. There have been other times I was thankful for brakes, when:

The car darted in front of me, too close.
The curve was sharper than I'd anticipated.
The semi-truck braked suddenly in front of me when I couldn't see what was ahead of it.
The animal ran into the road just as I appeared.
The steep grade was steeper than I was prepared for.

All these times, my working brakes saved me.

God also gives us brakes in life. There are times when His Spirit says "slow down" or "stop" what you're doing or just don't go wherever you're headed. Sadly, we often miss the signal or ignore the Spirit's warning, shoot ahead, and wind up suffering the consequences.

But here's really good news—better than having good brakes:

Even when we ignore God's warnings—He stays with us.
Even through the consequences of our poor choices—He helps us.
After we almost run the red light, or even if we do—He forgives us.
And He gives us grace to hear the Spirit's brake warning next time.

I'm thankful for brakes, especially the ones God provides.

Reading

ILOVE TO READ, AND I read everything except horror—the news provides enough horror for me.

I started before I actually *could* by badgering my mother to read to me. "I'll be so glad when you can read for yourself," I remember her saying.

I started reading independently in first grade and haven't stopped since.

One year I tracked how many books I finished and counted 365—I'm not making this up. Some I finished in two or three days, while the easier ones that I call "fluff" took only hours. Over the years I've lost count, but there are always new titles and authors to entice me.

Both fiction and non-fiction can teach; I've traveled with Dr. Seuss on Mulberry Street, experienced the battlefield in *The Red Badge of Courage*, and explored space in *A Wrinkle in Time*. I've visited New York City in 1880 and Chicago during the Great Fire of 1871, traveled the orphan train in the 1800s, and worked on an 1860 farm. I've solved mysteries in 1877 and stood beside Churchill during the Blitz of 1940–41. I watched Harry Potter grow up and learned about all sorts of things in this world and creation—and libraries let you do it all for free! So, take advantage and go on some wild adventures. Read!

Holy Sandpaper

I F YOU'RE ALIVE (AND I assume you are), you live among other people who are unique, with unique habits, opinions, and ways. Different isn't necessarily bad. We need different.

God gave Adam Eve because he needed someone "other"—not a clone. Similar—but not the same.

Kind, thoughtful people stretch us by calling us higher, encouraging us to be more patient and gentle like Jesus. And the ones who drive us up a wall? They stretch us too. I call them "holy sandpaper." A bit rough, gritty, and rub us wrong—but if we choose to see them as Jesus does, we leave a little more polished than before.

And the ones I dislike or who frustrate me—it may not even be their fault. It could be me. I know I've annoyed people without meaning to. We all have.

The people who challenge me can also teach me. They remind me that I'm not perfect and still need grace.

So, think of someone who gets under your skin—who really makes you twitch, who talks too loudly, is rude, or so self-focused they never consider anyone else. Now say a prayer for them.

Not because you or I are more spiritual or better, but because this is what Jesus—what love—requires. See them as God does. Because sometimes when we pray for someone else, God meets *us* instead.

Miracles

DO YOU BELIEVE IN MIRACLES? You should. They're all around you. Think hard—what miracles have you seen? Most people *see* them, but don't really see them. Want examples?

Paul and I were driving back from Massachusetts when, without warning, our car just died—lost power—while we were on a big bridge with a semi right on our tail. I prayed because I just *knew* that truck would smash into us and send us flying through the barricade and off the bridge.

Then—nothing.
(Since I'm still here, I bet you figured that out.)

We coasted to the end, pulled over, and lived to tell the story.

Another time, we were denied permission to go on a trip only to learn later that an earthquake hit the very day we would've been there.

And one more: I mailed a letter at the Air Force post office and said it needed to go the fastest way because we needed an answer in four days. The clerk laughed, saying it was impossible. I told him it would happen because we were sending it "Angel Express." He laughed again and shook his head.

Three days later? Our documents arrived. The same clerk greeted me, mouth hanging open. Over and over, he repeated that he didn't understand how it happened—that it *should not, could not* have happened. But it did. That's a miracle. They happen if you look for them.

Birds, Bees, and Flowers

I HAVE A BIRD FEEDER out back that Paul calls "Chez Brenda." I love to watch the birds. I've seen all sorts—cardinals, blackbirds, sparrows, finches, chickadees . . . and others I can't name. I enjoy watching them stuff themselves, even though they make a mess, tossing seeds all over the porch.

I don't see many bees but am grateful for the ones buzzing around my bushes in spring. I leave them alone, and they don't sting me—so we're both happy.

I enjoy flowers and plants, but they don't like me. The only ones I've had that have *not* died almost immediately—I think they commit suicide—are aloe plants. Or maybe the fact that I forget to water them factors into their quick passing.

Now, my mother? If she stuck a stick in the ground, it'd grow into a marvelous tree. Any living thing she touched flourished. But at my house? Expect to see plastic—artificial flowers and plants. So far, I haven't killed a single one.

So, even if I don't excel like my mother at gardens, I still have the birds. The pretty plastic flowers. The bees that keep their distance as they dance around summer blooms. It goes to show that on God's green earth—whether you live in a desert or the wooded South, and even if there's nothing on TV that day—look out back. There's always something to watch, to praise, and to help you pause and give thanks for today's tiny miracles.

Lost Things

I AM THANKFUL FOR LOST things. *What?!* I can hear you screaming.

Have you ever lost something and panicked? I've lost things that didn't hold much significance and could easily be replaced—glasses, jewelry, hearing aids, and my cell phone (okay, that loss was stress-inducing). But all these items can usually be replaced, often with a better version.

However, one day I lost my wedding ring and truly panicked. Yes, it could've been "replaced," but it wouldn't be the same. This was the ring my sweet husband gave me, the one he slipped onto my finger during our ceremony, engraved with our initials. The store where we bought it was long gone, and I have never seen another design like it. So, I panicked—intensely. I looked everywhere, sending up fervent prayers. After two days of searching, re-searching, and even throwing things out, I finally found it.

God continually reminds me (because I can be quite dense) that He is the One I should turn to in all matters, whether lost forever or temporarily. I also need to be more careful with my possessions. Truly, of all the things we "have," only people are irreplaceable. So, with a grateful heart, even if sometimes with reluctance, I thank God for the things I lose—because each lost item reminds me to pause, rely on Him, and treasure what really matters.

P. S. If you need to lose something, give it to me. I am an Olympic champion of losing things!

Joy and Memories

I'M REMEMBERING TODAY SOME OF my most joyous moments. Joy is different from laughter—although laughter usually comes with joy. C. S. Lewis wrote a book, *Surprised by Joy*, in which he traced his own spiritual quest from nominal Christian to atheist, and back to faith through a rediscovery of joy in Jesus. Sure, we all have good times and bad, but the joy of the Holy Spirit, the promise of our future, and the knowledge that God is walking with us—these keep us grounded and sane during this life. One day in heaven we'll experience unending joy. But for now, search your memories. Relive joy any time, any day, simply by pausing and remembering.

I think one reason we are so terrified of dementia is that we dread losing our memories. Good or bad—they shape who we are. Some I'd gladly forget, but others I'll treasure forever. When the world is finally restored as it was meant to be, will we keep all our memories of life on earth? I don't know. But today, rejoice in your good memories, and ask God to help you let go of the painful ones. I'm deeply grateful for my memories—especially the ones that include you, my friends.

Science

FOR MANY PEOPLE—CHRISTIANS ESPECIALLY—"science" has become a dirty word. But science is simply a tool: neither friend nor foe, neither good nor bad. It simply tells us what we observe in our universe—and what we believe based on *today's* understanding.

Some people also worship science, believing that whatever it claims must be true. But history has taught us otherwise.

Surprise! The earth isn't flat. And the sun doesn't revolve around the earth.

I'm never afraid of new discoveries because I know God is always in charge. He created and sustains this universe. No scientific theory can disprove Him—He built the earth beneath our feet and set the sun in the sky. God knew the earth wasn't flat, and He gave us the time to discover it.

So, when someone declares, "Science says . . ." and it seems to clash with Scripture, I don't feel threatened. Plenty of scientists are Christians, too. We shouldn't get upset or try to argue. We just have to wait for science to catch up. It often does. Because, after all, the Bible isn't a science textbook. It teaches truth through stories, metaphors, and the language of people who lived long ago.

In the end, science explains how *God's* world works, and faith gives us the guts to walk through it.

Death

TODAY, I'M THANKFUL FOR DEATH. I know that sounds odd. I am not actually looking forward to dying. In fact, I hope to postpone it for as long as God wills. What scares me is what comes before death—pain, suffering, and loss. I'm glad I get to leave all that behind when I finally pass into the glory of God's presence and His kingdom.

The apostle Paul said in 1 Corinthians 15:55, *"Where, O death, is your victory? Where, O death, is your sting?"* (NASB). In Jesus, we don't fear death because He conquered sin and death, and one day we will join Him. We'll live forever with God—a concept I can't fully comprehend now—in goodness and praise, in a state of perfection. That is far better than living forever on a fallen earth, suffering as my body slowly decays, my mind dims, and the world becomes increasingly wicked.

So, yes, it may sound strange, but I'm actually *thankful* God gives us death—because it points straight to the gift of everlasting life that follows.

I'm also grateful for the excellent medical care we have in the United States, like the kind I've witnessed while Paul receives his cancer treatment. The nurses and doctors have been so understanding and kind. I'm thankful for the dedicated individuals who look after our health, the technicians who keep track of everything, and the pharmacists who provide the medications we need. We are truly blessed—both in life and even in death.

Neighbors

ANOTHER THING WE SHOULD BE thankful for is our neighbors. Who is my neighbor? Jesus was asked this in Matthew 10:29. Remember how He answered? He told a story. If you don't recall it, look it up. Personally, I think of a "neighbor" as someone who lives close to me. Paul and I have lived in many different places and have had many good, helpful, and caring neighbors. However, we've also had a mix of neighbors, both good and bad.

Have you ever had a neighbor who drives you crazy? Perhaps someone who doesn't maintain their house or yard, is too loud, works on cars, raises hound dogs, is rude, or frequently complains about what you are doing or not doing? Is that person still considered a neighbor? What if they are of a different race or religion, or have a lifestyle completely different from yours? Do I still need to be *nice* to them? God, of course, says yes. Christians are called to treat everyone with loving and forgiving grace, regardless of their political views or church affiliations.

Consider the relationship between Samaritans and Jews; they didn't just dislike each other—they hated each other. Jesus came to eliminate hate and replace it with love. And remember, being a neighbor works both ways! Perhaps you're the "neighbor" who's driving everyone else crazy!

Small Pleasures

L ET'S TALK ABOUT THE GOOD things in life—our pleasures. If you think about it, every day brings us some pleasures, often little things that we take for granted. I'm not talking about grand experiences like vacations or buying something special. Consider the simple moments—the ones that just happen in life without you having much of anything to do with it.

Some of my favorites include: a hug or kiss from my husband; a piece of chocolate melting on my tongue; a cool breeze on a hot day; an uplifting word from a friend when I need it; a verse of Scripture that resonates within me; a hummingbird that hovers nearby; a note my late mother wrote long ago; sitting on the beach, feeling the sun and the breeze, listening to the waves crash and hiss; watching fluffy clouds drift by in many shapes; observing my dog, Peg, sleep peacefully; and reading a good book.

These are just a few of my pleasures. Yours may be similar or completely different. I encourage you to think about your small pleasures today. Maybe take a moment to write them out like I just did. But whatever you do, don't just let them slip away. Indulge those simple and small pleasures of life—you're worth it!

Unseen People

THERE ARE UNSEEN PEOPLE ALL around us—not literal ghosts, but those who blend into the background. We "see" but don't truly recognize them. They do their jobs with little or no thanks, minimal pay, and rarely receive recognition. The unseen.

Do you know the people who collect your garbage? Now, there's a fun job! Or the checkout clerk at the dollar store? What about waiters and waitresses, janitors, or mail carriers—people you rarely get to see until something goes wrong? Think of truck drivers, nursery workers, factory workers, salesclerks, the stockers in the supermarket—who always seem to be in your way. And the cashiers who ring you up—though they're a vanishing breed.

I'm sure you can think of others—people who keep the world spinning but rarely receive applause or recognition. They work for minimum wage day after day just to get by, to put food on the table, perhaps dreaming of more. We tend to notice them only when they're *not* there.

Next time you cross paths with one of these "unseen" folks, take a moment to say, "Thank you." It'll light up their day—to feel seen, appreciated. And if *you're* feeling unseen? Let me be the first to say: *thank you*. You matter. And I pray today many more see and appreciate all you do.

The Dark

W E NOTICE THE LACK OF light, don't we? I've gotten up and stumbled in the night. I even broke a toe once. We need light, and it amazes me how little it takes for light to illuminate the darkness.

In Virginia, we have Luray Caverns, a massive underground cave system. During a tour, when our guide cut the lights—it went dark. And I mean *really* dark; I couldn't see my hand in front of my face. It was darkness I could feel. Scary. Then the lights came back on, and everything was fine.

We crave light.

But when night falls outside, it's never pitch dark. The moon shines, the stars twinkle. Out in the open sky, they seem endless—but science says we see only a tiny fraction of them.

Psalm 8:3 marvels at the work of God's fingers in the heavens, and Psalm 147:4 reminds us that God calls each star by name—even the ones we can't see.

How can the God who created all of this care about us? He does. Jesus came so we could see through the darkness of life—those times when burdens pile up and we feel spent. Jesus understands. He walked in dark times, with far less light than we have now.

Sadly, many stumble in the darkness—sadness, cruelty, despair. But God has given us His light. No matter how dark it gets, His light is there, by our side.

Need vs. Want

I WANT A LOT, BUT deep down, I know I need less. Every day, God gives me exactly what I need. If He granted me everything I wanted—like some genie in a bottle—I'd turn spoiled, selfish, and self-centered.

But look at what He *has* given me: a wonderful husband, a sweet dog, good food, a nice house, a library full of books, and, yes, even a television to watch—though there's not much on that I really want to see.

James 1:17 says, *"Every good and perfect gift is from above, coming down from the Father of the heavenly lights, who does not change"*(NIV). God encourages us to ask for what we need, and He faithfully provides. Often when I don't get what I wanted, I realize my desire wasn't true gold—it could've caused trouble. Instead of answering my wants, He grants me peace.

It's all too easy to let our possessions possess us. People with abundant wealth and possessions can be unhappy—sometimes because they focus on *what* they have instead of *who* they are—and *whose*.

I am grateful He doesn't give me *everything*. God knows me better than I know myself. He cares for me and takes care of me. I have all I need, and I am content.

Pets

NOT EVERYONE IS A PET lover, but I am. I've had a wide variety of pets—lizards, turtles, hamsters, fish, birds, cats, and dogs—but it's the dogs and cats I remember best. I recall crying into my first dog's fur when things went wrong. My deepest sorrow came and still lingers for my beloved Basenji, the dog I bought and paid for and loved more than any other—until he was eaten up by cancer at just five years old.

Then there was Cookie, the little dog who bravely stepped between a little boy and a well-deserved spanking—because no one, not even his parent, could hit a child while she was in the room.

I can still see the joy on my mother's face when I gave her Tiny, the Chihuahua she'd wanted her whole life.

And Smoky Bear, our Siamese, brought me such comfort and cheer in Germany when I felt all alone.

Pets give us love without expecting anything in return. They give selflessly, even when their affection isn't appreciated, offering comfort and delight, grateful for the simplest things. Research shows that pets ease loneliness and boost well-being. That doesn't surprise me—I've lived it.

When you see a devoted pet, I believe you catch a glimpse of heaven.

Wealth

TODAY, I WANT YOU TO thank God for your wealth. What? You don't think of yourself as wealthy? Are you sure about that? Do you have food in your house? Do you *have* a house or apartment? Heat—or even air conditioning? Transportation? A job or income? Do you have friends? Family? A vehicle, car, legs to walk on—or even a wheelchair to take you where you need to go? If you can answer yes to most of those, then, my friend, you are wealthy. And every single day, you've got reason to be grateful.

Yet, many people measure their wealth by cash in the bank, the possessions they own, or what's in their 401(k). But I believe people in other countries recognize that wealth shows up in many forms, not just money. You can be rich and joyful with very little. It's all about how you look at what you've been given.

Jesus—the Creator of the universe—grew up poor. He didn't have what the world calls riches. But remember, our earthly world is owned by Satan—aptly named the Trickster. So, stop and reflect, and I think you will agree that you are rich in the things that matter. God will supply all your needs. So stop worrying, start rejoicing, and celebrate each blessing today.

Bible and Prayer

THE BIBLE IS THE MOST published book of all time—some five to seven *billion* copies printed over the centuries.

Do you have one? If not, they're easy to obtain. Just visit almost any church and ask for one. What an amazing book it is!

It has two main parts: the Old Testament, filled with history and law, and the New Testament, focused on Jesus—His life, resurrection, and the start of His church. Originally written in Hebrew, Aramaic, and Greek, it's now translated into hundreds (or thousands) of languages. You can even carry it in your pocket via a Bible app on your smartphone and never leave home without it.

Devotional books can inspire—but I am so thankful that I have the Bible to open, chew on, and search when I need guidance. Part of reading God's Word is praying, too. When I feel confused or my heart feels tangled, I ask God to reveal what He wants me to know and hear.

If you're new to the faith, the Bible can feel intimidating. If you haven't read it and don't have a guide, start with the New Testament—beginning with the Book of John. If you start with Genesis and try to push all the way through, you'll get stuck in Leviticus, Numbers, and Deuteronomy, with all their laws—*do this, don't do that.* It's helpful history, but it doesn't always speak to Christians today. Learn about Jesus and let God's Word guide your every step.

Senses

SENSES. WHEN I WAS GROWING up, I learned there were five: sight, hearing, smell, taste, and touch. Now science says there are more, like our "sixth sense," a.k.a. *proprioception*, which helps us know where our limbs are even in the dark. That's probably a helpful one to have! Are you thankful for each of your senses?

If even one is impaired, you'll notice immediately. If all of your senses are working—or most are—praise God. We often take sight and hearing for granted, even when we need glasses or hearing aids. And those who are blind or deaf? Their other senses sharpen over time—some even say they develop a "sixth sense" of awareness before something is wrong or about to happen.

We should all be grateful for what we have. A person isn't defined by what they possess—or lack—but by how they use what they've been given. So, rejoice in your senses. See in glorious color. Listen for every wonderful sound. Smell the good—and even the bad. Slow down and savor what's in your mouth. Feel the soft, rough, wiry, hard, and luxuriant textures of life. See, hear, smell, taste, touch . . . and feel it all with your heart.

Fear

TODAY, BE THANKFUL FOR FEAR.

Wait, what? Did I just say to be thankful for *fear*? Fear is awful—nobody wants to be afraid. How can we ever be thankful for fear?

Because fear is a gift from God for scary situations. It's our warning system. If a bear charges and you stand frozen as if nothing is going on, you'll probably get killed. Fear prompts you to *do* something—to run, fight, or hide.

But mindless fear isn't from God. He tells us not to be afraid—because He is with us.

Look at Bible verses like Joshua 1:9, 1 John 4:18, Psalm 23:4, Psalm 33:18, Psalm 34:4, Mark 16:6, Romans 8:15 and 8:31, Philippians 4:6–7—and many more. When God sends angels to deliver a message, the very first thing they say is, "Do not fear," or, "Do not be afraid." If I saw a large shining being suddenly in front of me, perhaps carrying a sword, I'd be afraid too. So, God repeatedly tells us to be careful and wise, but not to fear.

In a world full of things to fear, trust God—be wise, do right, and relax. God's got this—whether it's global chaos or your own personal battles. He has promised to return one day and bring everyone who calls on His name, Jesus, into His peace—and God does *not* lie!

Revelation

THE DICTIONARY DEFINES "REVELATION" AS the act of revealing or something that is revealed. The last book of the Bible is fittingly titled *Revelation*. You don't hear much about this book because:

1. It's scary.
2. It's confusing.

But John wrote it to give hope to suffering Christians. The book reminds believers that, ultimately, God wins, the devil loses, and we will live in a perfect heaven—far better than anything we can imagine. Revelation ends with Jesus saying, *"Yes, I am coming soon"* (Rev. 22:20 NASB).

Now, we've been waiting for about 2,025 years—so when is "soon"? The dictionary says "soon" means "without undue time lapse" or "in a prompt manner." For someone living between 70–110 years, "soon" implies a lot soon-*er*.

But God lives outside of time—an eternal being with no beginning or end—so, what is "soon"? Sooner than a billion years? "Soon" for Him doesn't match our human clocks.

Jesus understood our sense of time—He walked our earth in it. Perhaps our "soon" refers to when we die and go to be with Him.

I'm not worried. Jesus will return when He decides it's right, giving everyone a chance to turn to Him. Until then, the last book of the Bible provides Christians with hope: evil has an end, God will emerge victorious, and Christ's return is coming—soon.

Snakes and Spiders

TODAY, I'M THANKFUL FOR SNAKES and spiders—creatures I usually dread. But they do so much good. Without spiders, insects like mosquitoes, flies, and roaches would overrun mankind. And despite their fearsome reputation, very few spiders are actually harmful to people.

For some bizarre reason (maybe God's sense of humor), spiders seem to like me. It's like they look for me. Just ask me about the hotel room I had to evacuate one night at nearly midnight—it was crawling with all kinds of spiders. Then there was the oddly hairy, black-eyed one on a friend's doorknob just as I reached for it. I even snapped a picture to prove it!

I'm not a snake fan either, so I steer clear whenever I can. Still, if I spot one, I don't go for the kill. Snakes have a purpose too—they eat rodents and keep ecosystems balanced. I'm not inviting them in, but I don't kill them on sight either.

I'm thankful God created things I don't particularly like—because they still serve His purpose. So, if you see a spider or snake that's not hurting or threatening you, let it be. Letting them live reminds us that there's a design and purpose even in the scary parts of creation.

Another Thing

I BENT OVER TO TIE my shoes and suddenly thought, *That's another thing to be grateful for.* Many people—especially those my age—can't bend over to tie their shoes, or they have to do it carefully. I've been told the best way to bend is to squat down rather than bending from the waist, but how many of us actually do that?

How often do we perform simple tasks without even thinking about them, especially when we're young? Bending over, running, sitting down, getting up without effort or mechanical help, putting on jewelry or buttoning buttons without assistance—if you can do these, praise God. If you need help, praise God that you can still do them at all, even if it takes longer or you need assistance.

There are many things I can no longer do that used to come easily. But there are still many things I *can* do, and I'm grateful for every one of them. Focus on what you *can* do, not what you *can't.* You'll be happier. Stay healthy as long as you can. Do what you can while you can. And when you can't . . . deal with it—and thank God anyway.

Wear Your Mask

D O YOU REMEMBER THE DAY when the only people who said, "Don't forget your mask," were bank robbers? During the pandemic, everyone in public wore one—and if you didn't, businesses usually wouldn't serve you, and others complained. So many people were in the hospital sick—or even dying—of COVID-19. After the vaccines, when the worst of it seemed to pass, most of us went back to being "barefaced." Even today, some people still wear masks when they don't feel well or to protect themselves in a public place.

Paul and I recently took a trip. I wore a mask while in the airport and the entire time on the plane. Just trying to be careful. No one wants to get sick, and masks help, though they're not 100 percent foolproof. Wearing a mask is not a political statement, and it's not dumb. It's a bit uncomfortable, but if it protects us, our loved ones, or total strangers—it's the right thing to do.

Today, I thank God that He gives us ways to protect ourselves and others—not only masks but inoculations, pills, our natural antibodies, and more. He protects us from spiritual threats through His Spirit, through prayer, and by reading the Bible. If you need a mask, wear it. But even more important? Don't forget your daily dose of spiritual inoculation.

Cracks

IN MY NEIGHBORHOOD, THERE ARE lots of sidewalks—and walking on them feels much safer than dodging cars in the street. But there are also lots of trees, and those trees do more than offer shade: they also send out roots. Sometimes those roots push up the sidewalk where two blocks meet. When I walk, I have to watch for cracks that jut up. I've learned (after a couple of stumbles and a fall) to step *over* the cracks.

There are cracks in life, too. We're walking along, enjoying the view, when suddenly, we stumble or take a fall. The person we thought was "The One" turns out to be a toad. The career we'd dreamed of turns boring. Or the doctor says, "I've got bad news."

Stumbles. Falls. The cracks of life appear. But there is One who walks with us and holds our hand if we let Him. If you stumble, He holds you up. If you fall—whether bruised or broken—He lifts you and helps you rebuild.

You may never see the cracks coming. Just like sidewalks, you need to step over them. But if one catches you, don't panic—just reach for God. He'll be right there to hold you steady.

Candles

CANDLES ARE A FAVORITE OF mine, glowing with light in the darkness. I have many—mostly scented—and I just love the sight of that little burning flame.

But I'm super careful, knowing carelessness around even the smallest fire is a real hazard. A flickering flame that makes its way outside a fireplace or beyond the wick? I don't want that. So, I'm careful to set candles away from anything flammable, and I don't just blow out the match—I dip it in water.

I don't use candles as much in the summer, but in winter, when days are dark and dreary, having a sweet-scented candle burning feels wonderful. And it reminds me of our Light, Jesus Christ. One day there will be no darkness and no need for candles or fire. Revelation 21:23 tells us the glory of God will be our fire—our light in the darkness—and not only in the future but now. Nothing—no storm, no shadow, no doubt—can ever put Him out!

Today, while physical, mental, or spiritual darkness may still lurk around you, hold on to the fire that is eternal, the light that never goes out, the Spirit who lives in every believer. God be praised.

My Day

HERE'S MY TYPICAL DAY (MAYBE yours too): Get out of bed (thank God for the bed—and the sleep), take a shower (thank God for clean, hot water and soap), get dressed (thank God for clothes), fix and eat breakfast (thank God for food), get in a car or bus (thank God for transportation), and head to work (thank God for work)—or not (thank God for retirement).

During the day, you use the phone (thank God for communication devices), maybe watch TV, or listen to the radio (thank God for instant information and entertainment). Maybe you read a business report or a book (thank God you can read—and for paper, pens, and books). You chat with co-workers, friends, or neighbors (thank God for other humans).

Now I've only listed part of my day—and probably yours. What I've left out is more than I've put in. But how often do we just go about life, taking things for granted? We assume they'll always be there. That we'll keep doing what we've always done.

Lord willing, that may be true. But for many of us, there come sudden stops—interruptions, surprises—moments that force us to rethink our day, our world, and how we live in it.

If things go as expected, great. If they go even better, wonderful. And if they go badly, praise God anyway—He's still with you, right in the middle of it.

So, today, whatever it holds—make it a great one!

Stories

EVERYONE HAS A STORY. I thank God for the people I meet and the stories they tell. The longer you live, the longer your story becomes—and the more stories you'll hear.

I remember when we had no television—yes, I'm that old—sitting and listening to my mother and grandmother tell their stories: what it was like way-back-when, how they struggled as young people, meeting their husbands, and so on. It was like reading a book—but all true!

If you're fortunate, you'll meet all kinds of fascinating people with wonderful—even incredible—stories. But you have to be going slow enough, and be open enough, to actually hear them. Too many of us rush, rush, rush, and rarely take time to just sit back and listen to others.

The egotist and the fool are too full of themselves to stop and listen to others, so they miss out. But the wise know the true value of a life story.

Will you meet some boring people? Of course. But oh, the stories you'll hear. Be prepared to *stop* and *listen*. And be ready to tell *your* story—because you have stories worth sharing, and I look forward to hearing them.

Moments of the Day

MOMENTS OF THE DAY. THANK You, Lord, for giving us those moments each day—special, step-out-of-your-life moments. Like when I watch a blackbird fly to a very thin branch while the wind spins the branch up, down, sideways, and around, like some carnival ride. And the bird just holds on.

Moments when the sun is rising (or setting), and the colors are absolutely magnificent, reflecting on clouds. Or when it's high in the sky at midday and radiant sunbeams stream down through clouds—or through my window. Paintings only hint at how glorious it really is.

Moments when the world seems to hold its breath. Moments when I watch a tree in the wind—bending, swaying, giving way rather than breaking. It reminds me to give way sometimes, too. Moments when I step into the street without looking, and a car I didn't see sweeps past, missing me by an inch.

Moments when the waves come crashing in and hiss back out, the seagulls cry, and a cool breeze sweeps by.

Moments when the man I love says, "I love you," and holds me close.

Moments when, Lord, I feel *You* especially close.

Thank You, Lord, for giving me those moments in my day.

Hills and Valleys

HILLS AND VALLEYS—I'M THANKFUL GOD has given us both. Whether small hills or majestic mountains we struggle to climb—both are full of beauty and wonder.

Driving to and through the Virginia Blue Ridge Mountains, it's awe-inspiring to watch a faint blue line grow into towering peaks. I've flown over the Rocky Mountains all covered in snow. Impressive.

Valleys are best seen from the hills, but it's when you're in the valley that you really see its fullness. And then sometimes, when you're deep inside it, you can't see the whole picture.

These are physical hills and valleys—but what about the spiritual or emotional ones?

Everyone experiences hills: times when it's hard to keep going, things seem insurmountable, and every step exhausting. Then, once you've conquered your hill, you look back and rejoice.

Many Christians talk about "mountaintop experiences"—those moments when we feel especially close to God, when He shows us a glimpse of heaven and all the world's worries fade away. We long to stay there because going back means returning to everyday problems. Even the disciples who walked daily with Jesus wanted to stay with Him on the mountaintop (see Matthew 17:1–13).

God gives us those mountaintop moments to refresh us, to let us rejoice and bask in His glory. But we can't stay there. We're called back into the valley—where people are hurting, struggling, and searching for hope.

Thank You, Lord, for the times of refreshing—and for the call to return to serve.

Coffee, Tea, and Chocolate

I ENJOY MY COFFEE, ICED tea, and chocolate. Boy, do I thank God for these! I start my day with at least two or three cups of regular coffee. In summer, I drink a lot of unsweetened iced tea with meals—or just because.

And chocolate—I confess, I am a chocoholic. I can't seem to go a day without a little dose—candy, cookies, chocolate cream in a jar, ice cream, puddings, or hot chocolate. I *must* have chocolate.

Is that really true? No, not really. I enjoy coffee, tea, and chocolate—but I don't need them to live.

How about you—do you have something you enjoy that you don't really need?

I understand addiction (alcohol, drugs, food) better because of my deep enjoyment and strong desire for chocolate, coffee, and tea, but I thank God my habit is a harmless one. And, yes, I *can* go without when I need to. But some habits can be life-threatening—and they need to be faced and overcome. Thankfully, you don't have to do it alone. There is help both from God Himself and from others—people and organizations at the ready, offering support.

I thank the Lord He is there with me through every one of my sins—big or small. But today? I'm *really* thankful for chocolate!

Nicknames

NICKNAMES. WHAT ARE THOSE, EXACTLY? We all have names—our parents give them to us. We don't get to choose unless we insist on something different.

We name our pets and even things. But *nicknames*—those are special, human to human.

Friends—or enemies—can give us nicknames. Brenda becomes Bren; Elizabeth turns to Liz or Beth; James becomes Jim. My father was called "Mike" because of his red hair (still not sure why that made him a Mike!). And sometimes nicknames are just the exact opposite of reality—like a tall person nicknamed "Shorty."

The Bible is full of names that are hard to pronounce (Isaiah, Ezekiel, Zerubbabel, Artaxerxes), but can you imagine anyone calling Isaiah "Izzy" or Ezekiel "Zek"? Names don't define us—but they mark us. Nicknames? Whether we love or hate them, they dig deeper.

Want something truly special? Revelation 2:17 says God will give you a *new name*—written on a white stone, known only to you and Him. For us all, that name will be perfect, unique, and ours alone—because we'll be fully known and completely loved.

Quiz on Difference

WHAT'S THE DIFFERENCE BETWEEN HUMANS and animals, plants, insects, and planets?

We have a choice.

Plants follow predictable patterns. Animals are more complex, but (aside from humans) they're innocent—they *can't* choose. A lion can't wake up one morning and decide he'll be a vegetarian. A rose bush can't decide to become an oak tree. Granted, humans can't become lions or oak trees either, but we *can* decide who we'll be and how we'll act. Other creatures have no choice to change their nature—a lion is always a lion; a rose bush is always a rose bush.

God created a perfect world and gave humans dominion over it—to love, to live in, and to take care of it. And to humans alone, He gave the freedom to choose—to do good or evil, to obey or disobey, to follow God . . . or not. And what did we do? The first humans chose *not*. We were fooled, but we chose of our own free will. We decided not to follow God's desire for us and went about things our own way—and we've been suffering the consequences ever since.

Nevertheless, God loved us so much that after we told Him to get lost, He gave us another choice.

That's why we celebrate Easter: because God Himself—Jesus—died in our place. Animals remain innocent but bound to our sin—they have no say. But we do. Choose good or evil, God or self. Please, this time—choose right.

God's Protection

GOD PROTECTS. HIS CHILDREN ARE always in His hand, even when we don't feel that way. But God is there—because He promised, and *God does not lie!*

For example: My husband and I were driving home in a horrific storm, just a few miles from our house, when a huge tree limb came swinging into the windshield. We had about a microsecond to react before the windshield shattered. Somehow, we were able to keep creeping along unharmed, tiny shards of glass covering both of us. The car was scratched but not demolished. Another blessing—the insurance company covered the full cost, plus the rental car.

Another time, we had just ordered at a restaurant in Nags Head, North Carolina, when the ceiling fell. Literally! Fortunately, it wasn't busy, and where the ceiling came down (and I do mean *the ceiling*), no one was sitting—and no servers were underneath. After a few stunned moments, customers got up to leave. The owner said if we wanted to stay, we could eat outside (which Paul and I decided to do). After a delicious meal, the owner would not let us pay. He said it was on the house. We still love that restaurant. Just two examples of God's care.

Change

CHANGE. IT SEEMS TO COME whether I want it or not—and the older I get, the less I like it. Yet, I'm thankful, not always for the changes themselves, but that God allows me to adjust.

I think most humans are like me—we get comfortable and want everything to stay just as it is! Yet the only thing you can be certain of is that things will change. Seasons change, jobs change, even the weather changes—sometimes on the same day. Friends and family grow, go away, come back, die. Our favorite eating place closes or changes. A deadly virus hits (remember?) and everything changes—where we go, what we do, even how we dress.

Yet there is *one* thing, one Person, who never changes: God—Jesus—Holy Spirit, the Three in One. Read your Bible and you'll see: He does not change. He understands us, even as we change, even as we complain and pray for things to stay the same. But there is no "stand still." Even nature shows us that we either grow, or we die.

So, I thank God that He's there to help me through change—to make it the best change for me—and to stay with me if and when a hard change comes.

The Cell Phone

IT'S BECOME A CLICHÉ—BUT THAT'S because it's so true. Crowds at restaurants, walking down the street, at concerts or events—*all* with heads down, eyes glued to their cell phones. I'm from the generation that remembers not just rotary phones (black only!), but even party lines—where you picked up the receiver and listened for someone already talking, which meant you were supposed to put the phone gently back down and try again later.

I'm fussing—but here's the truth: I'm right there with everyone else, head down, checking emails, playing games, scrolling. I don't text or call while walking or driving, but yes—I am guilty of answering the phone when I shouldn't.

It's downright scary how tied we are to our phones and how we panic when they go missing or break. Our whole lives are on that device! Are you like me, and this seems wrong? Not that I'm giving up my cell phone—I mean, my whole life is on it! Sigh.

So, be patient with me and others who focus on a little screen instead of what's going on around us. And maybe we *can* remember to look up more often, like in the days before smartphones—just long enough to catch someone's eyes and smile?

Misunderstood

HAVE YOU EVER MISUNDERSTOOD WHAT someone said or what you were supposed to do? I have—often—especially before I got hearing aids. I would hear only part of what was said or think I heard one thing when it was actually something else.

Sometimes people get upset because they misunderstand or misinterpret another's words or actions.

For a short time at work, I had a trainee-helper. One day I walked in and it was clear she was upset with me. Our once-friendly work environment had turned tense. So, I asked her what was wrong. The day before, I'd left a note asking her to correct something. I thought nothing of it—we all make mistakes, and she was new. But in her eyes, I'd deliberately left that note out for others to see. I apologized for the misunderstanding and promised not to do that again. Just like that, our friendly atmosphere returned.

But suppose I had decided that since she was rude to me, l would be rude right back? The situation would've escalated, hurting not just the two of us but the whole office.

Be careful what you say and do, and if there's a problem, go directly to the person and try to resolve it. Or at least consider what they may be going through (divorce, a nasty child situation, medical issues, etc.). Remember forgiveness? God forgives us when we don't deserve it. We should try to extend that same forgiveness to others.

Taste and See

WE ALL NEED FOOD AND drink, and I've talked about that before, but I'd like to expand on it a bit. Psalm 34:8 of the King James Version of the Bible says, *"O taste and see that the Lord is good; blessed is the man that trusteth in him."*

Ever bitten into a rotten apple? Ugh! But it's a good thing you *can* taste when food's bad. Taste tells us many things—not only whether something is sweet or tart, spicy or bland, but also whether it's good or bad. Some people lose their sense of taste and have to force themselves to eat because, without taste, food brings little pleasure.

Swallowing. It's a simple thing—until it's not. Some have trouble swallowing food and have to puree everything. This morning, I'm grateful to say I took my pills with water, swallowed, and that was that. Then I had breakfast and coffee.

You don't need to thank God for each swallow but remember to be grateful when you can swallow without thinking.

How often do we gobble down food without tasting it? And how often to do we "gobble down" news or gossip without "tasting"—without reasoning or thinking about it, or considering how it's affecting us? God gave us both taste and reason, and He expects us to use them.

Sometimes poison is hidden in sweetness. So don't just "swallow" what everyone says, whether preacher, politician, friend, or otherwise. Ask God for wisdom.

Learning

D ID YOU HATE SCHOOL? I did. I loved to read, and school cut into my personal reading time. But I figured out that the quickest way to get *through* school was to just do the work, get good grades, and be done with it.

Funny—I actually do like to learn. You'd think I would have loved school. It wasn't the *learning* I disliked, but all the people I had to deal with to learn. Of course, even after high school, college, or graduate school, you never stop learning. There's always something new to learn—for your job, friends and family, hobbies, and just for your own enjoyment.

The most important thing to learn about is God. How? We'll never know everything, but we can start by reading the Bible, taking Bible classes, joining a church or Bible study group, and reading commentaries.

Maybe even just by being still, quiet, and concentrating on Him. Listen for that still, small voice speaking. Most of us are too *busy* in this world to actually slow down and listen.

Take a quiet walk. Sit and meditate. Read His Word and ask Him for understanding.

Will we know everything? No. But I don't think God minds our questions.

If you truly *seek*, you will *find*.

What's sad and disappointing is when we think we already know it all, when we insist everyone believe exactly as we do, when we boast and refuse to listen.

God offers. He never demands.

Windows and Blinds

TODAY, I'M THINKING—WINDOWS.

What's a house without windows? A prison. On a pretty day, it's nice to look out—but even better on a nasty one, when I'm thankful I'm not out *in* it.

Windows let us see everything that's going on around our house. They let in light. But windows work both ways. People outside—especially at night—can see us inside if we don't close the blinds.

Still, I rejoice that I *have* windows.

In a sense, God looks through our window—our heart. He doesn't need a physical opening, and no curtain can keep Him out. Be mindful of your windows—both physical and spiritual.

I close my blinds as the light fades to keep out the darkness and preserve the light inside. I open them every morning to let in the light of day. I thank God I have blinds that shut out dark and cold, yet welcome light and warmth.

Do we have blinds over our hearts?

Do we sometimes pull them down when we don't want to get involved in something—or someone's life?

Do we open them when God tells us to?

Maybe it's not our hearts we cover, but our eyes. Do we see only what we want or expect to see—and miss what's really there? Do we pull blinds down on the uncomfortable things we encounter in our everyday life? Blinds serve a purpose, but don't let them become a way to avoid what we don't like in our lives.

Forget

AND THE THOUGHT FOR TODAY is . . . I forgot!

Actually, that *is* my thought—how the older you get, the easier it is to start forgetting things.

With the specter of dementia hanging over us these days, anytime you forget something, it feels like a cause for worry. My mother—the sweetest woman who ever lived—forgot more and more until she even seemed to forget how to speak. She died at ninety-five, but in her last year, I never heard her say a word. She smiled a lot but never spoke.

So, when I misplace something or forget to do something, I sometimes feel a little panic.

That said, there *are* some things I'd actually like to forget—things I've said or done in my past that I'm ashamed of. And I believe that once I'm in heaven, I won't remember those past sins. God says He forgives *and* forgets. As far as the east is from the west, that's how far He throws our sins from us—and we should follow His example.

How many times have you said or heard, "Well, I may forgive them, but I'll never forget"? But if you don't forget, did you truly forgive? Or are you holding on to that sadness, bitterness, anger?

And here's the surprise: holding on to your hurt or anger will not affect the person who harmed you at all.

You are the one who will suffer.

So, just let it go. Give it to God. Forgive—and forget.

Nasty People

I AM GRATEFUL FOR NASTY people. Wait—say what?

Most of us are more than grateful never to meet nasty people—those who complain, make snide comments to or about you, or do annoying, irritating things (not evil, just . . . unpleasant).

Things like shutting a door in your face, degrading something you said, or deliberately trying to belittle or shame you.

So, how can you be *thankful* for such people?

Because it gives me (and you) the chance to respond with kindness, love, forgiveness—what they don't expect and what they may rarely see.

We are told to turn the other cheek instead of replying in kind.

Where do you meet these people?

They're everywhere—even in church sometimes. Now, don't think I'm a saint who always responds with love. I can strike back verbally—and often do. But if I can respond with Jesus's love, I'm thankful for the opportunity to be a witness for Him. It's not easy. I'm human. Still, with God's help, sometimes I succeed.

I'm thankful the Holy Spirit lives in me—helping me become better than I am and helping me to grow spiritually. So, yes, I'm thankful for nasty people. They help me grow.

Let's Sing

I LOVE TO SING—BUT DOUBT you'd enjoy it if you heard me. My voice is okay, but not great. Still, I do love music—and I love hearing others sing.

When you listen to a song or any music you enjoy, something inside of you just wants to jump up and move. If you've seen me swaying and jumping at church, now you know why. There's a song for whatever you're feeling—worship, sadness, fear, confusion, loneliness, gratitude, love. Some are newer gospel or spiritual songs; some are older, familiar hymns.

And it needn't be Christian music. Even secular music can touch your heart and lift you up.

I love classical music—often feeling like I'm soaring into the heavens when I hear an orchestra. My husband, however, is a rock-and-roll kind of guy. On our first date, he took me to a Harry Chapin concert—folk music, which we both enjoy.

Church music has always lifted people up and inspired them, often giving a voice to what they feel but can't quite express. God even provides music with wind in the trees, songs of birds, and the hum of everyday life. Sometimes, though, we need a bit more.

So, if you're feeling sad or depressed—put on some music.

COVID-19

THE COVID-19 CRISIS TAUGHT ME many things. One was the value of Zoom and other ways to communicate remotely. Paul and I were retired when COVID-19 hit, so we didn't have to work remotely or go into an office. Yet we—and many others we spoke with—still felt so isolated.

Everyone wore masks or stayed home. Friends might call on the phone but didn't stop by. We did our grocery shopping by sending in a list, paying with a credit card, and driving for pickup when ready. We didn't even get to *meet* the person who shopped for us. He or she would place the groceries in the back of the car, say, "Thank you," and we'd drive off.

Even churches were closed. We watched services on television.

You don't realize how important that personal touch is—until it's gone. Humans are social creatures. We need interaction with others.

Paul and I called people often, watched a lot of television, read a lot of books, walked outdoors where we could at least see and wave to neighbors. Eventually, the danger lessened, science found a vaccine, and life became normal again—for the most part. Sadly, COVID-19 and other diseases are still out there, but God is still on the throne. I'm grateful we survived lockdowns, and now I'm even more grateful for the little things we can do again, like actually talking with the neighbors and going to get our own groceries.

Losing Weight

M Y WEIGHT. *UGH.*

When I was young—even into my mid-thirties—I had no problem with weight. I ate whatever I wanted, whenever I wanted.

And I *loved* sweets: candy, cakes, pies, pastries, puddings . . . almost anything chocolate and/or sugary is my downfall. *Still.*

But the older I get, the harder and harder it is to shed those pounds. I've dieted, lost the weight—only to gain it back when I return to eating whatever I want.

Part of this is my lack of exercise. I read. I don't jog. I don't go to the gym. I even have trouble walking on a regular basis.

So, who can I blame?

TV—for showing all those delicious-looking foods?
The store—for stocking shelves full of sweets?

Maybe.

No—the harsh truth is, I am to blame. Although honestly, I think "blame" is too harsh a word. We get older. It gets harder to lose weight. We don't exercise enough. We eat too much—or eat the wrong things—and we gain.

But even if I cave in to a gooey dessert or refuse to exercise, God loves me no matter what I weigh or how I look.

My husband loves me, too—just as I am.

I'm still trying to exercise more and eat less, but I don't obsess about it. I know I'm loved. And that's what's important.

Work/Jobs

G ENESIS 2:15 TELLS US THAT when God created Adam and Eve in the garden, He gave them a job: look after the garden and take care of it.

Remember the old saying, *"Idle hands are the devil's workshop"?* Apparently, those first two weren't busy enough!

God made us to work—to *do* something.

I think part of the world's problem today is that all people think life owes them a living. They find themselves hating what they have to do to earn money. Yet everyone does some kind of work they enjoy, even if they call it something else: a hobby, a sport, a calling, recreation—or (for those wise enough to choose it) their actual, cash-earning job.

God intended us to work—but to do what we *enjoy*. And that makes it not work but pleasure.

Unfortunately, as we do with many things, we've turned something God meant for good—the God-given desire to *do* something—into drudgery. I'm thankful to be able to do something I enjoy. If you're still working and hate it, find another career—or do something you love in your off-time.

The happiest people I know are those who are still "working," still active, right up until they leave this earth.

The Little Things

ARE YOU THANKFUL FOR ALL the little things?

I started this daily blog to remind myself (and a few friends) to be thankful for the small, everyday blessings we so often take for granted—and expect to always have.

Like the hug of a loved one. A bird's song. The exquisite taste of chocolate. Opening our eyes in the morning and getting out of bed (without pain, I hope).

Being able to walk, talk, and read. Greeting friends, family, and neighbors. Devouring God's Word without fear. Speaking with the Creator of the universe—anytime, anywhere. Breathing without effort or thought. Living without pain—or at least having medication that helps.

Not everyone is free to do all these things. And the older I get, the harder some seem to be. Even walking is a challenge these days. But God is still in control—and His plan will succeed.

Whenever I start to feel sorry for myself because of my little aches, pains, or worries—I think of people like Christopher Reeve, Stephen Hawking, or Joni Eareckson Tada.

They not only overcame incredible challenges but also inspired the rest of us.

We may not become famous or do great things. But we *can* do all the little things for ourselves and for others that make the world a better place.

Laughter

L AUGHTER IS GOOD. UNEXPECTED LAUGHTER is the best—even if it's at your own expense.

Thank You, Lord, for laughter, even when everything seems dark.

An example:

Lately, I've been having eye problems, so I really need reading glasses to see clearly. I sat down to read a book and couldn't find my glasses. Paul hadn't seen them either, so he got up to help me look.

He checked the dining room, my office, the living room—even the kitchen and bathrooms. No glasses. Neither of us saw them anywhere.

I finally went to another room and got another set and sat back down at the table to read and eat breakfast.

I dropped a little egg on my lap (I'm not the neatest eater), so glanced down to make sure it didn't stain—and guess what I saw! That's right— my glasses.

I had tucked them into my shirt so I'd have them when needed. It's like putting them on top of your head and then searching frantically . . . or talking on your cell phone while digging through your purse to find it so you can check your calendar!

Okay, I'm not the brightest bulb in the universe—or even the neighborhood. But I laughed and showed Paul—who had looked right over them too!

God is good. He gives us little ridiculous things to laugh about—to remind us He's there. Don't take life so seriously. Laugh. It feels good— even when you're laughing at yourself.

Problem-Free

ARE YOU PROBLEM-FREE? No? ME neither. We fuss, complain, and probably pray that God will solve all our problems.

God—Jesus—is the answer to our prayers. But sometimes He seems far off or simply answers, *"No."*

Why?

Perhaps because He knows more than we do.

Perhaps our problems are what's molding us into the person He wants us to become. Maybe our troubles can help someone else, now or in the future. Maybe our concerns are bringing someone into our lives whom we need . . . or who needs us.

To us, our concerns are immediate. Our rescue feels urgent. We need help *now*. But God sees time, the world, and us—differently. It may take months or years or a whole lifetime to understand. We all have problems. Some serious, some small, but all feel important to us.

Give them to God, and rest in the truth that *He understands.*

Remember the apostle Paul? A great man—yet even he had a "thorn in the flesh" he begged God to remove. But God said, *"My grace is sufficient for you, for my power is made perfect in weakness"* (2 Cor. 12:9 NIV).

God helped Paul deal with his thorn. And He will help you (and me) deal with ours.

Appliances

EVERYONE—RICH OR POOR—USES some kind of appliance: laundry machines, stoves, refrigerators, vacuums, microwaves, a grill, a juicer, a television. Maybe—tucked back in your garage—is even a bread maker for all those fresh-baked loaves you were *going* to make.

Machines are just another thing we take for granted in this fast-moving world.

I remember helping my mother do the laundry when I was a child.

First, we'd drag the washer into the kitchen to connect it to the kitchen faucet. Then, we'd gradually load the clothes into the tiny machine. After washing, Mother would feed each piece into the wringer to squeeze out the water, and I stood on the other side pulling. Don't know how many fingers I got squashed in that thing, but it was a lot.

Actually, this next part of the wash—I miss. We'd go out to the backyard, and I'd daydream while hanging the clothes to dry, enjoying the fresh air, birds singing, trees rustling, and my mind far away.

Afterward, everything smelled so good and fresh and clean—no dryer sheet comes close to that smell. Then we'd unclip them from the line, fold and place the clothes in a basket, and drop the clothespins back in the holder. That part also took a few trips in and out of the house.

Mother always told me how *easy* we had it compared to when she helped *her* mother with the laundry.

This is why I thank God for appliances.

Donkeys

I HAVE ALWAYS BEEN "HORSE crazy." I like to watch them, ride them, groom them—even clean out the stalls. Majestic animals: useful, beautiful. As many recent books point out, mankind could not have accomplished half of what we've done without them.

Donkeys are small, useful, not particularly beautiful, and definitely not majestic. Yet, they have a purpose. They're also more affordable and easier to maintain.

Donkeys are mentioned in critical scenes throughout the Bible: Balaam's donkey saved his life—not just once, but three times (see Numbers 22:21–39).

Jesus knew and used donkeys. His mother is often portrayed as riding one to Bethlehem. Jesus rode one into Jerusalem to announce the coming of His kingdom.

Donkeys, unlike horses or mules, are usually unassuming—just doing whatever they're asked to do. I'd never refer to a person as a donkey because they'd misunderstand and think I'm insulting them—when really, I'd mean it as a compliment.

I've known many Christians who were unassuming, who didn't look for credit or praise—who did unglamorous jobs simply because they needed to be done. They serve the Lord however they're needed, but don't seek recognition or awards.

Yet God sees them—just as He sees the often-overlooked donkey. Horses are beautiful. Mules are helpful. But donkeys are special.

Discoveries

HAVE YOU MADE A DISCOVERY today? I'm glad I can still discover things. One thing that's wonderful, and can be scary, about toddlers is how they're always discovering things. Watch them like a hawk, because when they see something new (and everything is new), they reach for it, put in their mouth, feel it, maybe throw it. Toddlers are explorers, and every day is a new adventure where they are confused, amused, frightened, and thrilled by things we know all about and take for granted—those everyday things we are so used to that we forget to be amazed.

God gives us mysteries and waits for us to discover them—planets, stars, flowers, birds, a vaccine for a virus. All through mankind's short time here on earth, we've been discovering things. We started with fire and its uses. Today, it's spectacular, almost constant, new discoveries. When something new is found, whether it's something we personally find out or a new technology or breakthrough, we have two ways to look at that discovery: prideful and arrogant—"Look what I (or humans) have done." Or in gratitude—"Look at what God has revealed to us."

The second is a more true and better way to look at new things. Personally, I look for a new discovery each day. It's a treasure hunt.

Lost

HAVE YOU EVER LOST SOMEONE or something that you loved? Do you feel a gap—a hole—where they used to be? Does it hurt?

Of course it does.

Yet, loss of people and things is part of life. Should we be thankful for that? Yes—because loss causes growth.

Loss teaches us empathy for others. It pulls us closer to one another and to God. Of course, for some, the pain is so deep they pull away instead of drawing near. Sadly, they try to lock themselves up so they'll never be hurt again. That doesn't work.

Physical things—items—are easier losses to recover from because things can be replaced, but people can never be replaced. I'm so thankful for their impact on my life and that I have memories of them to hold close.

And there are other kinds of loss:

The loss of a marriage.
The loss of trust in a friend.
The loss of a reputation.
The loss of a job.
The loss of a pet.

Losing is not something we enjoy. Even Jesus knew loss. His earthly father died sometime after He was twelve. Some of the people He invited to follow Him turned away.

But those of us who have trusted Jesus with our hearts know this: all our losses will one day be restored—a million times over. The Bible is full of people who suffered loss . . . and were blessed. When you lose something precious, turn to God.

Handy People

NEITHER PAUL NOR I ARE what you'd call "handy." Even the simplest things that break can seem beyond fixing for us. And if it's something serious—like the roof or the garage door—we stand in amazement as a neighbor or a repairman/woman fixes it.

Now, we do have our talents, but being handy isn't one of them. And I confess—Paul is better at fixing things than I am. When something breaks or stops working, I yell for him. And if he can't fix it, we call a friend or neighbor. And if they can't fix it, we phone a specialist—and pay for it. If you can fix things—great. Feel good about yourself.

Sometimes, when we try to "fix" something we're not equipped to handle, we just make it worse. I think most of us are worse at fixing relationships. So often, we let people drift out of our lives—or cut them off—for good or bad reasons. The only expert I know to call on who can truly fix relationships and friendships is God Himself. So, when I have a problem with a person, I take it to Him.

Of course, in relationships, both parties have to come together, and that doesn't always happen. Then I just give my friend, co-worker, or associate to God and let them be.

If something breaks—don't call me. It's just not my talent. Now, if you need someone to walk your dog or read a book . . .

The Good Life

THE GOOD LIFE.

What does that mean?

I think it's something everyone wants—but we all have different ideas of what it *is*. What makes *"the good life"*?

Plenty of food and drink? Entertainment? Good health? Healthy and obedient children? Never worrying about money? Getting whatever you want—whenever you want?

Is that truly the good life?

Then why do so many rich people seem so unhappy—always trying to find something new, something exciting—or just more money?

No. The good life is one with God.

Since He's the Creator, He understands us in ways that we don't even understand ourselves. When we search for "the good life," we're really searching for Him.

When life gets hard, when things fall apart, we may cry and complain. We look for someone or something to blame. God understands this. Remember the Book of Job in the Bible? Job had everything—and he gave God thanks. Then, he lost everything: his family and wealth—even his health. His friends assumed it was his fault—that Job must have sinned.

Job didn't understand either. At first, he praised God. But after much suffering, even he began to doubt. Then, God reminded Job who'd given him his blessings—and who was really in charge.

Because of Job's faithfulness, holding on when all seemed lost, God restored everything to him . . . and much more.

When you give everything you have to God, you cannot lose it—and the devil can't take it away.

The Church

THANK GOD FOR THE CHURCH. The global church (all denominations included)—which recognizes God as Three in One: Christ the Savior, Holy Spirit, and Father—was created to tell people of His love, to comfort, and to strengthen.

The first church was mostly Jewish with a few Gentiles. But as it grew, Gentiles saw something different, something wonderful—and soon outnumbered Jews as *"the church."*

Sadly, the more people who joined, the more the church grew secular—concerned with appearances: what status you held, how a certain ceremony should be performed. People started believing the performance mattered more than the Lord.

Christ's church is to be one—to uplift not only the Lord but each member.

I have a shirt that says, *"The church has left the building."* It reminds us that "the church" is not the building but the people inside. We are to be helpers, comforters, encouragers to each other—as well as examples to those outside the church.

Sadly, so many people today have a wrong or twisted idea of what "church" means. Read 1 Corinthians 13. It's a short chapter. The church is one body united against the devil-controlled world, yet loving the people of the world, letting them know of God's love and forgiveness, available to any who ask.

I'm thankful for my church—the people who encourage, correct when I drift away, and who let me support them at times. We stand together—ready to do Christ's will and help each other.

How to Bathe a Cat

TODAY WE'LL LEARN HOW TO bathe a cat:

1. Very carefully.
2. Pay someone to do it.

Bathing a dog is a lot easier. They don't love it either but they're better behaved. And they don't scratch . . . *much*.

I've had many great cats in my life: BoBo, Missy, Smokey Bear, a kitten that ran away. Smokey Bear was a purebred Siamese. She was the most dog-like cat I've ever had. I could take her anywhere. She rode on my shoulders like a fur wrap or walked on a leash. She protected, loved, and even washed me down sometimes.

I want to tell you a story I read or heard somewhere. I didn't invent it, but I love it.

Have you heard about the creation of dogs and cats?[1]

God (before Eve, apparently) felt Adam needed a companion to stay with him, love him forever, and help him with chores. God said, "This companion will love you no matter what."

And God created Dog.

But after a while, an angel said to God that Adam was getting full of pride because the dog loved him too much—no matter what he did.

So, God said, "No problem. I'll create another being—one who will be with him forever, who will see him as he is, will remind him of his limitations, and ensure Adam knows he is *not* worthy of adoration."

And God created: the cat. *(Haw!)*

Okay, you could've substituted *wife* for *cat*—but I prefer cat.

---

1. "And God Created . . . Pets." Accessed July 4, 2025. https://mobile.ghanaweb.com/GhanaHomePage/fun/jokes.php?ID=2767.

Angels

AT CHRISTMAS, I HAVE ANGELS scattered all over my house—ceramic, fabric, porcelain. I have a large one that I made myself in ceramics class. My favorite is a cheap wax angel. One year, I found her *melted* a bit. Her head had turned to face backward instead of forward. She also had a green bow stuck to her backside! It looked like she was looking at it saying, "What is *that* stuck to my bum?"

Angels are interesting creations. The good ones we call angels; the bad—we call demons. Every time an angel appears in the Bible, their first words are, "Fear not." Why? Probably because the sight of an angel is *terrifying*. God can disguise them to look human—but they're not.

When Joshua faced an angel who apparently looked human and asked, "Are you for us or for our enemies?" the angel replied, "Neither, but as Commander of the Army of the Lord I have come." (See Joshua 5:13–14.)

Angels obey God. They help us—because God tells them to.

I suspect angels are as amazed as we are at how much God loves humans. Angels are powerful beings, but we should never forget that they serve God first, not us. And that *we* are to serve and worship God—not angels.

Day of the Lord

THANK YOU, LORD, FOR THE "Day of the Lord."

What is the Day of the Lord?

Well, it could mean the day Christians honor God and gather together to worship Him. For most of us, that's Sunday. It could also mean that day when Jesus returns for His own—what is called the "Second Coming." It could be the day you accepted Jesus as your personal Savior, or it could mean Easter, the day we celebrate the rising of Jesus.

Christians look forward to and celebrate the Day of the Lord, in whatever meaning it holds. But I think the Day of the Lord is *every* day that we draw breath here on earth. Every day, we should thank God for that day—whether the day felt long or short, good or bad, perfect or imperfect.

What we have now is another twenty-four hours (okay, sixteen if you get eight hours' sleep) to show people *who and what God* is, and ... —

To be a reflection of Him;
To do good works;
To help and support others.

After all, aren't we called "Christians"—"*little Christs*"? God has given us another day to spend time with Him here on earth. Rejoice! *This* is the Day of the Lord!

Vacations

I LOVE VACATIONS WHETHER THEY'RE long or short. When we were young and had no money, our vacations were always local—or we went to Massachusetts to visit Paul's folks.

A vacation is time to get away from the regular routine, to do something different—somewhere different, to let go of all worries and fears and just enjoy yourself.

It can be as close as another city or as far away as Europe—as simple as a short car ride to visit a local site, or a long cruise down the Mississippi.

Disney World? The Grand Canyon? Washington, D. C.? The Bahamas? The local museum or historical site? Every place has some interesting or historic site. And if you can't afford to leave for whatever reason, you can also take a vacation by bringing out old albums, pictures, or videos of previous trips. Zoom or call relatives and talk about trips you've taken together. Or maybe just sit down and plan a future trip—even if it never comes to pass. You can have a whole lot of fun just thinking about your next dream vacation. And thank God that no matter where you go, there's no place in heaven or on earth where He is not.

Shyness

I'VE ALWAYS BEEN SHY AND uncomfortable with strangers. In school—mostly middle and high—I had few friends and no boy-friends because I was too shy to say hello to a boy. My brain froze and tongue tied whenever a boy approached. I didn't have my first date until I started working.

But as I've grown older, meeting people has become easier. They're only strangers until you get to know them. And most people are very nice and understanding.

Part of *my* problem is I'm so bad with names. I remember faces, but it takes me a *looonnnngggg* time to connect the face with the name. And I'm so embarrassed about it, I pretend I remember—which is awkward. And the older I get, the more I can suddenly draw a blank on people I've known for years. Embarrassing. Sigh. Shyness makes me stand in the corner at weddings, funerals, church get-togethers. It makes me reluctant to jump into new activities. I'm still trying to be more outgoing. When I find the courage, I enjoy meeting new people and situations. But it's still hard. So, please forgive me if you meet me and I can't remember your name or where we met. It's *not* deliberate. It's just me.

And I'll do the same for you. If you happen to forget my name, and if I even notice, hopefully we can have a laugh about it and rejoice in the fact we remembered each other's faces!

My Mother

MOTHERS ARE SPECIAL. I THINK just about everyone agrees on this—although mothers are as different as the rest of us humans.

There are all kinds.

I was blessed with a saint as a mother. I was about eleven, Sandra about four, when Mama and Daddy divorced. Mama became the sole parent and breadwinner. She called on her own mother to come live with us, to "handle" us children while Mama worked in a factory. She'd work hard all day, come home by bus, eat, help me with homework, and act as referee between my sister and me before collapsing into bed.

Repeat every day but Sunday, when we'd go to church.

Then one day, when I was a teen, my grandmother had a massive stroke. Mama was met by neighbors and an ambulance. That's when we went on welfare. Mother took excellent care of her mother for the rest of her life—putting a hospital bed in the main bedroom while the three of us slept in one bed in another room. Mama cared for us all—cleaning, cooking, giving her mother better care than any hospital or nursing home could have provided.

There's not enough space to tell all the wonderful things she did and was. God gave me the most wonderful mother a girl could ask for—far more than I deserved. She was ninety-five when she died, and I still miss her. But I will see her again—with all her rewards—in heaven one day.

Holidays

HOLIDAYS ARE MEANT TO BE enjoyed—even if you do nothing but "nothing."

Have you ever thought that every holiday is a reason to be grateful—for *something*? I'll mention a few, though I know there are more.

First, our own personal birthdays—when we celebrate ourselves! Or those we love.

Mother's Day and Father's Day—thankful if we had a mother or father, especially if they were one of the good ones.

President's Day—for all the good presidents we've had, and for having survived the bad ones.

Memorial Day—to remember all who fought for us in so (sadly) many wars, and those who gave their all—their lives and their future—so the rest of us could go on.

Labor Day—being thankful that we have jobs, money, and the ability to work.

Fourth of July—when we celebrate our nation.

Thanksgiving—when we remember all the things we are thankful for (though we usually just eat and drink a lot).

Christmas—when we celebrate the greatest and first Love: God's love for us in sending us salvation in His Son. When there was no possible way we could reach up, He reached down.

As much as you are able, celebrate each holiday as it comes.

Glasses, Contacts, and Seeing

ALL MY LIFE I'VE BEEN nearsighted. No matter how small the print, I could read it. But anything more than a couple feet away turned blurry. As a child, I would sit about three feet from the TV and get yelled at. They'd make me move back. Slowly, I'd inch up until I could see—and get yelled at again.

I did a lot of sneaky inching—until the first (or maybe second) grade, when every child was vision tested. When asked to read the eye chart, I could see nothing but blurs. That's when I got glasses. Suddenly—I could see! All those blurry, colorful shapes became actual objects. The world was real—and I could *see it*! I've never forgotten that miraculous moment.

I wore glasses through my childhood, teens, and early adulthood but, in my twenties I went with contacts. They worked great once I learned how to poke myself in the eye. At sixty-five I decided I was tired of contacts and went back to glasses (bifocals)—until I needed cataract surgery.

I asked the surgeon if he could give me both far- and near-sighted lenses. He said no—I had to choose. I chose to replace my natural lenses with far sight. Today, I can wake up in the morning and *see*!

The downside? Now I need reading glasses.

This world is never perfect. But praise God—one day we'll have a world, a universe, that's better than perfect. One day.

Unexpected Pleasures

HAVE YOU EVER EXPERIENCED THE *unexpected* pleasures of this world? I'm sure you have.

When someone gives you a gift for no reason.
When you take a walk and it's a perfect day.
When you step on the scales and discover you've lost a pound—without even trying.
When a friend or relative you haven't seen in a while calls or stops by.
When you're shopping and you find the perfect outfit.
When your cat drops a mouse at your feet.

Okay . . . maybe not that last one.

I think children are better at noticing these moments than adults. They expect nothing from the day, so they're often—and usually—joyful with whatever they find.

For instance, Paul went to the library and spied a little girl about three or four years old in pink boots, happily stomping about in a rain puddle—her mother smiling nearby.

Sadly, when we become adults, go to school, get a job, maybe get married, have children—in essence, we "grow up"—we lose this ability to see and appreciate the unexpected pleasures that come to us each day.

Today, be on the lookout.

I'm sure you'll spot at least one—if not more—of the little joys you didn't expect.

Earworms

I KNOW EVERYONE WHO READS this has encountered an earworm—and hated it. You're going along, all happy and innocent, and you hear a song. It might be one you like—or one you can't stand—but it's a song you know and, somehow, you've heard it a thousand times. And then . . . it gets stuck in your head.

It stays with you for minutes, hours—even weeks!

It repeats in your head endlessly. Before you know it, you find yourself singing or humming it.

Congratulations. You've got an earworm.

I googled the term. Apparently, more than one hundred years ago, Germans coined the phrase to describe the experience of a song stuck in the brain. And no matter what you do, you just can't make it go away.

What's worse, once you start humming or singing—bingo! You've passed on this little earworm.

Row, row, row your boat.
Silent Night
Maybe a rock-and-roll song from your youth.

Earworms aren't harmful. Just annoying. Usually, we don't even realize we've been "infected" until somebody tells us to stop. Too bad we can't pass on kindness or love this easily. The world would be so much better.

Anyway . . . watch out for the earworm. *Happy birthday to you . . .*

Coloring and Painting

REMEMBER AS A LITTLE KID how you liked to color? Some of us didn't even use books. Walls, doors, floors—whatever we felt needed a crayon mark.

And all the coloring books! I loved the ones with horses or other animals. I loved coloring.

About a year ago, one of my friends—an artist—volunteered to show anyone interested at church how to paint. A bunch of us started.

Tonya and many others in our class are true artists. I'm a dabbler. I do landscapes because my birds, animals, and people end up looking like alien invaders or cartoon characters.

Landscapes—flowers, trees, oceans—look *mostly* like they're supposed to. Now I've got a ton of paintings stacked up around the house.

But I really, really enjoy painting. It's not only relaxing—it's a joy to watch something recognizable appear from a blank canvas.

I wonder if that's how God views us?

We're born, we grow, and what we see, do, and how we're raised determines what kind of human picture we'll be. If we let God—the Original Artist—help, we turn out beautiful. If we try to do it all on our own . . . it'll be a brownish mess.

There may be an artist in you. Give it a try. And if not painting or drawing—maybe a coloring book? They have them for adults now. You never know what you can or can't do until you try.

Courage

Anthony Clement McAuliffe was the commander of the 101st Airborne Division defending Bastogne, Belgium, during World War II. When surrounded by enemy troops who demanded his surrender, he replied, "Nuts."

I like to imagine the Nazis' reaction: "Nuts? Does that mean yes or no? Is he asking for supplies?"

Courage is a hard word to define. There's the dictionary meaning, of course, but there are so many ways humans exercise and display courage.

We show courage in war—which often looks like being terrified, expecting to die, yet fighting on.

The courage to stand up to a bully—especially when you're sticking up for someone *else*.

The courage to refuse to stay silent when you know something is wrong—risking danger and personal cost just to do and stand with the right thing.

Courage to invite a stranger to church, knowing you may be rejected.

Having courage doesn't mean you're not afraid.

In fact, to me, the person who is afraid, maybe even terrified, but does what they know is right, is the bravest of all. And none of us are brave all the time. Sometimes, we let fear win. That doesn't mean you're a coward. It just means you're human.

Nuts

D<small>O YOU LIKE NUTS?</small> I do.

I'm talking about the food kind—not your crazy neighbor.

I love all kinds—pecans, walnuts, peanuts, cashews, and so on. But my favorite is macadamia nuts. Of course, they happen to be one of the most expensive, so it's a real treat when I get them.

Nuts are good for you but, unfortunately, many people are allergic to them. I'm not sure whether that includes all nuts or just certain types, but it's sad to think there's a good food you can't eat.

You can eat nuts by themselves or toss them in with other foods. Cracker jack? Nuts on a cake or in a pie? I even have a recipe for green bean casserole with nuts.

"Nut(s)" as a word has many meanings and not just as a "hard-shelled dry fruit or seed." Look it up sometime!

It can also mean "nonsense" or refer to a foolish or eccentric person—among other meanings.

Usually, when I have company over, I like to put out some fruit, nuts, and candy (for those who aren't watching their weight).

Nothing really serious today—I just wanted you to know . . .

I like nuts. Hope you do too.

Perfect, Beautiful Day

I REMEMBER THE HECTIC DAYS of working.

I'd wake up, throw down breakfast, get dressed, jump in the car, get to work, work, eat lunch, drive home, fix and eat supper, maybe watch television or read—and then fall into bed, only to do it all again the next day.

Even weekends had chores.

Yet, when I was a child—and now that I'm retired—I love to *experience* the day, especially a beautiful one.

What makes a beautiful day?

Well, that depends on who you are.

For me, the perfect beautiful day is when the sun is shining and there are just a few fluffy white clouds drifting by. There's a cool breeze blowing steadily, softly, to blow away the bugs while I sit on the porch. The temperature is about 70–75 degrees Fahrenheit, and I have a book I've wanted to read in my hands.

Flowers are blooming everywhere—on trees, bushes, and from the ground—perfuming the air. Neighbors walk by with their dogs and say hello. I have no urgent plans, no place I must be, no aches or pains—nothing to do but relax and enjoy being alive. That, to me, is the perfect, beautiful day.

What's yours?

Pain

Pain.

No human likes pain—whether in the body, mind, or soul. Pain is a signal that something is wrong. And I hate to say it, but physical pain is a good thing.

When you hurt, when you have an ache or some hidden injury, your body is alerting you—there's a problem, something you need to fix, pay attention to, or take care of. And when we ignore pain, it usually gets worse.

But pain isn't just physical.

We also carry pain in our emotions, minds, and souls. We feel pain when we remember something we regret but can't fix. We ache when we miss a loved one who has died. We suffer when a friend suddenly turns on us, especially when we don't know why.

Pain comes from many sources.

We feel the urge to fix, to get rid of it—but sometimes, we can't. And in those moments, all we can do is try to cope, numb, or ignore it.

But when you have pain you can't fix—give it to God. The Creator of all things heals all. He can take your pain away—or give you the strength to endure it. Remember the apostle Paul and his "thorn in the flesh"? For a reason we don't know—God allowed it. It was painful for Paul—but, apparently, it served a purpose.

I hope and pray you are not in pain today. But if you are, know this: you are not alone.

Treats

MY DOG LOVES TREATS. SHE doesn't care whether it's cut-up carrots, Kix cereal, a store-bought dog treat, or something we had for dinner. All we have to do is say the word, and she's there in front of us, dancing—which is hard for a three-legged dog to do—begging, saying, *"Give it! Give it!"*

I think we all like treats.

We like them because they're special and unexpected—a surprise! A treat! Something extra that we didn't plan for or see coming. And it doesn't always have to be food. I get a treat when a new book by a favorite author is released. Paul gets a treat when the Red Sox win. You get a treat when (you fill in the blank).

How dull the world would be without surprises—without the occasional treat. Yet, if we give our dog, Peg, too many, she gets fat—which isn't good for a three-legged dog—or for anyone, really.

Treats cease to be treats when you get them all the time. No more surprise. No more unexpected delight. Once they become predictable—even expected—they stop being special. No longer true *treats*.

So, enjoy the treats you have—but don't expect to get them all the time.

Expert

I'M AN EXPERT IN . . . NOTHING. I know a lot about many things, but I'm no expert. Some people are experts in their field, in a hobby, or on a subject they love.

We need experts—people we can turn to when we have a need:

How to cook something.
House repairs.
Car upkeep.

And especially when it comes to our health—we definitely want doctors and nurses to be experts.

Teachers are experts in many things. They have to be, to teach.

What are you an expert in? Are you like me—someone who knows a lot about many things, but still wouldn't call yourself an expert?

Wait—actually, I take that back.

I can type. I'm an *expert* typist.

I learned to type in school on an old manual (QWERTY) keyboard, and I'm a fast, efficient typist—which is exactly what I'm doing right now.

Maybe you're like me—at first, you think you're not an expert.

But think some more.

I bet you *are* an expert in something. Don't people call on you to ask about—whatever *that* thing is?

We need experts in life, but not everyone needs to know everything. You just need to know where to look. Where to find an expert. That's why we have the internet, dictionaries, libraries—to discover what we need to know.

Count Your Blessings

I ENJOY THE COMIC STRIP *Pearls Before Swine* by Stephan Pastis. The man is truly either a genius—or strangely strange. But he makes me laugh. In one strip, Rat, who is always negative, is complaining about how lousy his day is. Goat, the optimist, suggests he try counting his blessings. So, Rat goes off to do so and comes back with *minus* blessings!

Do we do that? Instead of counting our blessings—what we *do* have and what *is* good in our lives—do we focus on what's wrong, what we don't have, or what never happened?

I try in these daily wanderings to remind each of us (me too!) how many good things we *do* have—how God has blessed us, even when we struggle or face frightening times and situations.

God is good—all the time. Sometimes clouds drift over us and keep us from seeing the sun, the good, in our lives. And sometimes storms do hit, tossing us and our hopes around, making everything seem dark. But even in storms, the sun is still shining above—and it *will* come out again. So, when you count your blessings, don't be a Rat and focus on the negative. Realize that no matter how bad everything seems right now, God is with us, and He has a future for us—a good one.

Hold on.
Remember past blessings.
Look for new ones.
Know you are not alone.

Fire Alarms

I HAVE A QUESTION:

Why do fire alarms *always* start chirping at midnight—or very, very early in the morning?

This morning, we had two go off. We stood in the middle of the house, waiting, anxious. *When* and *where* would the chirp sound?

There it was! We ran to where we thought it was (we have about ten—I'm paranoid about fire).

We stopped. Waited. No—it's in *that* room, not this one.

Finally, we found it, went out to the garage to get the ladder, pulled the alarm down, and took the battery out. Then ran (okay, walked) upstairs to get a new battery. And while Paul was doing that, I heard *another* chirp.

Sigh.

It took almost twenty minutes, but we finally got both batteries changed.

Both my husband and I are "getting on" in years. These days, any time either of us gets on a ladder, it's scary. So, I decided that my Christmas present for my husband this year will be to hire someone to change all the batteries in the smoke alarms for us. And you know what? A friend just told me—firemen will come and do it for free. All you have to do is call and schedule. And they are *experts*!

Art

WHAT DO YOU CONSIDER "ART"? I enjoy visiting museums and seeing all kinds of art. But some things in museums—though called art—don't appeal to me, personally.

"Art" can mean different things to each of us, depending on what we enjoy or connect with. For me, art is anything I consider beautiful or thought-provoking. It can be a painting, a photograph, a drawing, a sculpture, a quilt, a handmade item, a symphony, or a song that moves me. Whatever speaks to me, that means something or stirs something inside—that invites me to look past the obvious, or to just appreciate what's there in plain sight.

God gives people talents to create beautiful things. And of course, God is the first and greatest Artist. Mountains. The ocean. Birds. Mammals. The morning sky or evening's sunset. The pouring, pounding rain. Rainbows. A horse in motion. A pet's devotion. And so much more.

All are beautiful in their place. Every person He creates is different, likes different things, and moves through life in different ways. Each day, I try to keep my eyes open for the "art" in all things around me—both natural and man-made.

Sometimes we focus too much on what's wrong, what's ugly. Look today for the art that is there—all around you.

Tongues

MANY PEOPLE MISQUOTE 1 TIMOTHY 6:10, saying money is the root of all evil. But that's incorrect. Scripture actually says, *"For the love of money is a root of all sorts of evil"* (NASB, author emphasis added). Money is a commodity—neither good nor evil. But the *love* of money, riches, possessions, things . . . this can become your god. To worship this false god, you find yourself doing things that are *not* good.

The Bible is full of sayings about money: Hebrews 13:5, Matthew 6:24, Romans 13:8, Luke 16:14. I especially like Ecclesiastes 5:10: *"Whoever loves money never has enough; whoever loves wealth is never satisfied with their income"* (NIV).

Is this not true? We've seen millionaires and billionaires who cheat, steal, and lie to get more. It's not the money or wealth. It's about putting your love in *things*—not God.

I wholeheartedly agree with Psalm 16:6: *"The boundary lines have fallen for me in pleasant places; surely I have a delightful inheritance"* (NIV).

My husband and I have been blessed. We have enough. We're not rich, but we're not poor. I grew up poor, on welfare, and I know the difference.

Always remember: none of us actually owns anything. One day, you'll leave this earth and take absolutely nothing with you. Hold what you have lightly. Give from your bounty—to friends, to enemies, to charities. God expects you to be wise in how you give. Just don't worry about it. He will keep you.

Need Help?

HAVE YOU EVER NEEDED HELP? I have—and if we're honest, all of us do at some point. Some of us have no problem asking for help when we need it; others are very reluctant to admit they need it. They could be drowning but insist they can swim!

There's an old saying, "When the going gets tough, the tough get going. The not-so-tough scream for help." That's me—screaming for help in just about everything. Who do I ask? Parents, children, friends, neighbors, church members, the pastor, my husband, the government . . . my dog (but she's really no help at all).

There is one Person who is always there, always helping, no matter what the problem: God. Maybe He won't come and fix your roof, but He might send someone who can. Prayer is a Christian's most powerful weapon, and no matter what the problem is, He can fix it—or help you endure it. And Christians help each other. In the early days of Christianity, that was one attribute that made them so different, that made them stand out. They helped each other—even when they'd receive nothing in return, or when it was dangerous to do so. Christians help, even when it's undeserved.

Bookmarks

E VER BEEN READING A BOOK and dropped it, or closed it and forgot to mark your place? Isn't it a pain to find where you left off?

That's why I'm thankful for bookmarks. I have all kinds: magnetic, plastic, ribbons, fancy, plain, ones with Bible verses or funny sayings, cheap cardboard (usually sent with a request for a donation), and on and on. I have a lot of bookmarks.

And when I need one but discover none is within reach, I use a piece of paper, a receipt, an unused tissue, or, once, a dollar bill. I do *not* like losing my place.

Bookmarks enable one thing—picking up in your book exactly where you left off. I think we also have markers in our lives: reminders that signify something important, something we don't want to ever forget.

The ancient Hebrews knew the importance of remembering. When something significant happened, they'd put up an Ebenezer, usually a mound of rocks, to be a visual reminder for all generations. Don't we do the same? All over the world, you can find statues and monuments. God taught His people to do that so they would remember their choices and the outcomes that came from them.

And yet, even with markers, we still forget. Nations and peoples still make the same mistakes. Sad.

Today, if you see a marker reminding you of something from "yesterday," be sure to learn from it today.

Christmas

GOD IS GOOD, AND WE should always be about His work—but—we are human (at least, I am). And sometimes a person just wants a break—to sit back, rest, be entertained, and take our minds off ourselves and the condition of this world. I read books to "escape," but I also watch television. I avoid social media, which tends to be chaotic and not helpful.

For example, although Christmas is not real close, the other day I binged on Christmas movies. I watched five, one right after the other. Some were great. Some were okay, and one was so bad I stopped after fifteen minutes. The sad thing—for me, anyway—is that none of them tied Christmas to Jesus. The stories were all about good feelings, being nice, Santa Claus, giving to others, love for family or for a particular person. All these things are good—but *not* the reason for the season! Not about the birth of an infant a little over two tousand years ago.

When I watch Christmas movies, I do enjoy them, but the best are those that remind us of why the holiday is celebrated. Not so kids can have toys, not for holiday parties, not for feeling good for a few days, not to relax and take a vacation. Christmas (see the name?) is to celebrate Christ—a God who cared enough to enter our space and our world because it was the only way to reconcile us to Him.

Merry Christmas.

Be Nice

I'M A CHRISTIAN. I DON'T deny it. I'm rather proud of it, and occasionally, I even act like a Christian. We're supposed to be nice. Actually, we're supposed to be better than nice, but niceness will do if that's the best we can manage. I try to be better than nice, but if I'm having a really bad day, nice is enough.

What is nice? Not shouting or pouting because things are not how you'd like them to be. Saying "please" and "thank you." Holding a door open for someone behind you. Helping a short person reach something on the top shelf. Not yelling at kids that are really annoying or are in your yard. Forgiving your spouse or friend for the millionth time when he or she does something that annoys you. You're being a *real* Christian if you forgive and do not mention it.

I've met people who followed a different religion than Christianity. They were nice. They were better than some professed "Christians" I have known and worked with. And that's sad.

"Nice" actually comes down to what Jesus said. Doesn't everything, eventually? Jesus said to treat others as *you* want to be treated. If every Christian was nice every day, I think the world would notice.

Passwords

D O YOU HAVE A PASSWORD? Actually, if you're like me, you probably have a lot of passwords. Or you let AI automatically generate and remember a password. It's sad that we live in a time and place where you have to be so careful, locking your information up with a "pass"-word to keep it from crooks. And even then, sometimes they get your password and damage you—or your purse.

Did you know early Christians had a "password"? Since many of Jesus's first apostles were fishermen, the password for Christians was the fish. The devil was doing all he could to stomp out God's salvation before it could spread, so people were being thrown in prison, killed outright, or thrown into the Colosseum for entertainment—then death. Yet what Satan planned for his purposes allowed Christians to be witnesses, and Christianity grew.

A password allows someone access—entry into a file, a group, or a building. Revelation talks about a day when Jesus returns to take back His own. The password for heaven is the Holy Spirit, given when we accept Jesus as our Savior. This password is open to all who want it and cannot be stolen or twisted.

Cars

D O YOU HAVE A CAR? I recently had to renew my driver's license, which was an interesting experience. I understand how hard it is for those of us who are "getting up there" in years to have to give up our car or driving altogether. You get used to thinking, "I'd like an ice cream," then hopping in the car to go to the ice cream shop or grocery store for a pint. You can get around without a car, but it's not easy or convenient. Whether you use a public bus or call for a ride service, you still have to wait and pay (although it's probably much cheaper than a car's upkeep).

But even if you're still driving and you have that car, you must be careful. I've seen people run red lights, thinking, *I can beat that yellow if I speed up*. I've seen them breeze right by a STOP sign—*Oops, didn't see it*. Or drive too fast for the area, busy calling or texting on their cell phone rather than watching the road.

If you're still driving, good for you—but please obey the rules. Look out for other drivers as well as pedestrians crossing at odd times and places, often wearing black at night, loose dogs, and frightened deer. Don't think driving is easy because it isn't. And with electric cars, you can't even hear them coming!

Favorite Toy

A SK ANY CHILD ABOUT THEIR favorite toy and they'll tell you not only what it is, but why. Did you have a favorite toy growing up? I think we all did.

If the family didn't have money for store-bought toys, you made them. I made "toys" out of pots and pans. They became wonderful musical instruments—until Mother took them away. I've mentioned how much I liked to color. A piece of paper and a crayon or pencil opens up a universe of possibilities.

I used to get under the dining room table—covered in a long table-cloth, of course—and imagine I was in the jungle or in a cave. Kids have great imaginations. Sadly, many of us lose that when we get older. And sometimes, I think giving children too many toys actually cuts back on their creativity.

There was a small, undeveloped wooded area near my house. I used to spend all day in there, imagining all sorts of adventures.

What about today? Do you encourage your child to imagine? Do *you* create—imagine what could be, what might be? So many great inventions came into being because someone said, "Why not?" I believe any of us who are young or young at heart still find toys to play with, to enjoy, and adventures to explore. What are yours?

If you enjoyed this book, will you help me spread the word?

THERE ARE SEVERAL WAYS YOU can help me get the word out about the message of this book . . .

- Post a 5-Star review on Amazon.
- Write about the book on your Facebook, X, Instagram, LinkedIn—any social media you regularly use!
- If you blog, consider referencing the book, or publishing an excerpt from the book with a link back to my website. You have my permission to do this as long as you provide proper credit and backlinks.
- Recommend the book to friends—word-of-mouth is still the most effective form of advertising.
- Purchase additional copies to give away as gifts.

The best way to connect is by visiting
WhatGodSeesBook.com